ASTON'S BUILDING BLOCKS

Written by

Catherine Wilkinson

Illustrated by

Angela Mingledorff

DEDICATION

Dedicated to my little man.

ABOUT THIS BOOK

These books are designed to be interesting for your child. I hope that they will find it interesting to learn about the different emotions and things that they can see in their world. With these books and also the SELIA Kids program, my aim is to promote an introduction to emotional, cognitive and environmental awareness. Research has shown that a foundation in awareness can lead to better choices, decision making and problem solving. And that these can lead to a more fulfilling life for the individual and the people around them.   Part of the importance of learning these skills is the practice of slowing down to become aware of and acknowledge what is happening around us.

Often so much is happening in our lives and our children's lives that children can get over stimulated and overly involved in the situation without realising. The danger in this is that behaviours can happen that are not healthy, or sometimes not how we would usually have liked to have behaved ourselves or have had our children behave. When we become over stimulated and bombarded with information, be it social, environmental, relational, or emotional, we start to lose the opportunity to think and make decisions.

Critically we lose the opportunity to learn the skills we need to live healthy and fulfilling lives. Often we don't realise we do not have the right skills to use within the challenging situation until we really need them! This is exactly what these series of books are designed to do, to teach your child and open the communication lines to develop strong social and emotional skills. Skills such as resilience, confidence, teamwork, leadership, self discipline, delayed gratification, and emotional regulation.

You will find as you spend time with your child with these books, and implementing the techniques, that your relationship with your child will change. You will notice your own understanding is improved, your child is more responsive, and your relationship will be strengthened. The questions within the books are designed to promote conversation in general, but also to set a precedent of your child feeling comfortable in talking with you about their feelings from a very early stage where your relationship is the most important one in their life. Please use the questions as a prompt, though expand and add your own experiences to connect with your child where possible. I hope that you will enjoy them too!

Catherine Wilkinson   BA (Psych)(Hons), Dip Prof Couns, Cert Frontline Management, Cert 1 Trainer, ...and Mum!

Aston has a set of building blocks. He loves to play with them all the time.

Do you have building blocks like these?

They are all different colours and shapes. There are blue squares, green rectangles, yellow circles, and red triangles.

What shapes can you see?

Sometimes he likes to stack all of the same coloured blocks together.

What colours can you see?

He also likes to try and build a GREAT BIG castle. He stacks the building blocks one on top of the other, up and up as high as they can go.

What do you think might happen?

But sometimes when he builds them up, he accidently knocks one over and the whole castle comes tumbling down.

Point to them.

When this happens, Aston feels frustrated because it is not working how he would like it to.

Can you see how Aston feels frustrated? How can you tell? Let's have a look...

His eyes are close together with his eyebrows pointing down in the middle and his jaw is clenched tight.

Point to them. Can you show me your frustrated face?

And his hands are bunched up really tight like a ball.

Do you remember a time when you felt frustrated? maybe when you were trying really hard to do something and it just wasn't working? What happened?

Aston felt so frustrated he just felt like screaming really loud! Oh dear! He ran to his Mummy, "the blocks aren't working" he yelled!

Aston's solution was to run and tell his mum.

Mummy could see that Aston was feeling a little frustrated, "Would you like some help?" she asked. "Yes please", said Aston. Together they went to rebuild the castle.

What could you do when you feel a little frustrated? Brainstorm some ideas.

SELIA KIDS PROGRAM

SELIA Kids is a division of the Social and Emotional Learning Institute Australia (SELIA). It is an opportunity for parents and carers to connect with their children and teach them the vital skills they need whilst growing in these critical stages of development and especially towards starting school. Skills for development that they will carry through into adolescence and adulthood.

The Social and Emotional Learning Institute Australia (SELIA) was founded to establish social and emotional learning (SEL) as a fundamental part of child education. We operate a multi faceted approach working with families with children from 0 to 6 years through our **SELIA Kids** program, and working with principals and leaders from primary schools throughout Australia. Our consultants and program developers work with advisors in the United States, the UK and New Zealand to ensure up to date and established SEL practices.

SELIA is *Putting the Pieces Together* for child academic, social, and emotional education.

Social and emotional learning (SEL) is a strategy for developing the essential life skills necessary for greater success throughout all the different aspects of life. SEL builds the skills we all need to manage our lives, our relationships, and our study or work, more effectively and with greater satisfaction. Skills such as recognising and managing our emotions, making responsible decisions, handling challenging situations constructively, and establishing fulfilling relationships.

In respect of children, these skills help them to understand what they are feeling and make appropriate behaviour response choices that further help them to keep themselves safe and resolve conflicts or confrontations more effectively.

The Collaborative for Social and Emotional Learning (CASEL) has identified five core groups of social and emotional competencies:

· *Self-awareness*—accurately assessing one's feelings, interests, values, and strengths; maintaining a well-grounded sense of self-confidence

· *Self-management*—regulating one's emotions to handle stress, control impulses, and persevere in overcoming obstacles; setting and monitoring progress toward personal and academic goals; expressing emotions appropriately

· *Social awareness*—being able to take the perspective of and empathize with others; recognizing and appreciating individual and group similarities and differences; recognizing and using family, school, and community resources

· *Relationship skills*—establishing and maintaining healthy and rewarding relationships based on cooperation; resisting inappropriate social pressure; preventing, managing, and resolving interpersonal conflict; seeking help when needed

· *Responsible decision-making*—making decisions based on consideration of ethical standards, safety concerns, appropriate social norms, respect for others, and likely consequences of various actions; applying decision-making skills to academic and social situations; contributing to the well-being of one's school and community

Please visit our website at www.seliakids.com.au

or for primary school educators www.selinstituteaustralia.com.au

All Titles in the Series:

Elle-Sue Doesn't Want to Play
Aston's Building Blocks
The Circus is in Town
The Surprise
Just Looking

www.ingramcontent.com/pod-product-compliance
Lightning Source LLC
Chambersburg PA
CBHW060813290526
45792CB00005BA/1636